WESTERN SWING

Also by Andrew Greig

POETRY

Men On Ice (Canongate, 1977)
Surviving Passages (Canongate, 1982)
A Flame in Your Heart, with Kathleen Jamie (Bloodaxe Books, 1986)
The Order of the Day (Bloodaxe Books, 1990)

MOUNTAINEERING

Summit Fever (Century Hutchinson, 1985)
Kingdoms of Experience (Century Hutchinson, 1986)

NOVEL

Electric Brae (Canongate, 1992)

WESTERN SWING

ADVENTURES WITH THE HERETICAL BUDDHA

Andrew Greig

BLOODAXE BOOKS

ISBN: 1 85224 268 X

First published 1994 by
Bloodaxe Books Ltd,
P.O. Box 1SN,
Newcastle upon Tyne NE99 1SN.

Bloodaxe Books Ltd acknowledges
the financial assistance of Northern Arts.

Cover printing by J. Thomson Colour Printers Ltd, Glasgow.

Printed in Great Britain by
Bell & Bain Limited, Glasgow, Scotland.

Yes we'll catch
that wisdom train
but why arrive
so early at the station?

— BUD

Thanks to:

The Scottish Arts Council, whose Travel/Research Grant made Morocco possible.

Norman MacCaig, whose enthusiasm for this multi-verse (so far removed from his own brevity and clarity) was crucial encouragement towards completing this (and whose Glenmorangie gave rise to 'Stella's sampling').

Dr Philip Hobsbaum who asked 'What is the true voice of an educated East Coast Scot of your generation?' until I found an answer. (Many voices.)

Rory Watson and Edwin Morgan, for their time and support and craft.

And Mum for the Shed, and Marj for the love, again.

The High Atlas section of *Western Swing* was a prizewinner in the 1993 *Observer*/Arvon International Poetry Competition. Parts of the poem have also appeared in *Chapman*, *The Observer*, *The Observer Arvon Poetry Collection* (Observer Books, 1994), *Poetry with an Edge* (Bloodaxe Books, new edition, 1993), *Rebel Inc*, *Spectrum* and *Verse*.

WESTERN SWING

Adventures with the Heretical Buddha

PROGRAMME NOTES

Some of these characters appeared in more mythic roles in *Men On Ice* (Canongate, 1977), which was mostly staged imaginatively in the Himalaya. This new longpoem may be considered a late sequel of sorts. Further sometimes helpful Notes & Acknowledgements are provided at the back of this Programme by 'Ken, the Reader's Friend', and may be referred to now or during the Intermission between Acts II and III. The Insomniac's Bar-and-Kitchen remains open throughout.

DRAMATIS PERSONAE

'I': Narrator, reader, witness. Also the Company as collective. Also Ananda (see end notes), Drew. An empty vessel.

Ken (formerly *Grimpeur* in *Men On Ice*): as in 'you ken' or the philosopher Anthony Kenny: a knowing man, the doubt-filled intellect. The head.

Stella (formerly *Poet*): The scene-setter, a troubled young woman, the heart.

Brock (formerly *Axe-Man*): A surly badger or Pictish stronghold. The body, and its music.

The Heretical Buddha (formerly *The Bear*): Who's he? If the three principal characters were legs of a stool, the *Heretical Buddha* would be the seat. And I would be the one who tries to sit on it.

But already the lights are going down...

PART I The Quest & The Company

*Darkness. The sound of the sea. As eyes adjust we become aware of a
reading lamp, a solitary reader, a bed, and a few signposts. Such as:*

PROLOGUE

A solitary speaks

I am afraid
There is much to be afraid of

Bad enough on good days
when jolly fishermen strip legs from living crabs
and you wince how that must feel
and glimpse how quick we're guddled
from first cry to last gurgle

Worse: waking alone
in a large bed in a small country
with a pain in your chest
and the sea going on and on
like the auld haiver you'll be

if you're spared

*

I am afraid of many things
I could make a list
but it would go on a bit
That list would fell a rainforest

Sleep's out of the question
and you might as well admit it
make tea and sit up in bed
with this sapling's worth on your knee

and roll a cigarette because though you're afraid
you refuse to be intimidated
and it's some sort of friend
touching your lips now –

*

'A mate at the cricket club
in the shower after the game
felt a lump on his shin

Bone cancer
Cut off the leg
Waited

He came to spectate
propped on crutches on the boundary
Then they took the other one

From a wheelchair he
watched the last match of the season
Said we'd have won but for a terrible decision

After the funeral
we had a whip-round for the wife and kids
What can you do?'

but stare out the window of the 4.32
like the man who told me this
as we glimpsed the cricketers

      resolving
          their lunar-solar, luna sola
game

*

If the human heart
were a high and mighty bluff
set above a smashing sea
with a nearby rail link into the city
and excellent local facilities
plus opportunities for education and shopping
and a really nice cricket ground next to the cemetery
wouldn't you call its potential for development

– unlimited?

And we have seen it wasted
on yet another grotty scheme

Utterly unmortgageable at four in the morning
you lean on the windowsill
pain in the chest but still
calling the bluff

and hear at last the sea make sense
the sense you began to make
when you finally owned up and said
'I am afraid'.

This is as good a place to start as any.

* * *

So roll that log, old pro!
a new voice whispers, soft and delible.
Call him the Heretical Buddha, HB.
He speak in ital and he say
Make your contribution and then fade...

Prologue ends

LIGHTS UP DIM

Scotland. January. Snow.
A mean day gloomily
shutting up shop. We see
a rusting questing 2CV
shoogle over Black Mount
wi two last-minute customers...

'This salted road's a black tawse
whacked down on Rannoch Moor.'
Crack! The wiper blade breaks off.
That'll learn ya, son,
                 the Buddha spat
then with a sigh leant out and cleared
the windscreen with his brolly.
Anthropocentrism makes you blind,
             a kind
of beating your own trumpet.

He huddled deeper in his cloak and warmed
to his subject
          (which was as well
          for with the window open to permit
          the passage of his brolly
          it was bloody freezing as I
          steered towards another slide
          of tense and personnel
          that lie across our way like ice)

Might as well call the punitive tawse
a strip torn off the A82, your palm
this land in miniature.

I hold out my palm and wait.
At length Bud shakes his head,
       gently places
my fingers back upon the wheel:

I read: a violent culture,
great wilderness in the heart.

Above the whirring shoe-box
a hoodie craw veered North,
I scanned for something dead or dying,
thought of my friend Donald,
HIV positive, two tendons cut
by a Stanley knife when he came in
on my account when I was
jumped by Casuals in Queensferry
between the Chinese and the chippie –

'Sure thing,' I said, 'but mine own.'

The white palm dipped beneath the blow
and we declined towards Glencoe,
hands tight and careful on the wheel.

It's narration of a sort
when someone salts the road for us
and lets us whirr past Buchaille Etive Mor
to wind down like a clock
and stop
                    outside the Clachaig Inn.

'Let's enter. I have friends here.'

A Short Aside

Who reigns here?

You'll be noticing a tendency
to change name, sex and destiny
not to mention subject, season and location,
and if this history runs on iron rails
it's only those of sound and rhythm
while the sweaty driver whistles
samples from all eras
as he whacks new vocals
down those gleaming tracks –

Who reigns here? I say the door of the Clachaig
opens on a street in Kathmundu; say
and we are walking with the Heretical Buddha
at dusk, past Hindu shrines
where fruit bats like inverted priests
hang in dusty eucalyptus trees;
incense, spice and sweet-sour piss,
odours of sanctity churned
by passing bicycles, the wind stirs
in merely mentioned trees
and we –

Slam that page shut! Later...

You take the point.
This is not the concrete world
and everything here
                              bends
(when you incline your ear)
faster than plastic when you credit it.

Got all that? Good. Knew
you would.

End Short Aside

Now back at the Clachaig,
two customers wait upon their Quest
for better beer and synthesis, and we
can dispense with leaden formalities
such as 'the real world'.

Let's simply say
Inside the Clachaig Bar

and we are.

          – 'Hey, Drew! Whit ye wantin here
             besides the company of friends
             and hope of ace ice action
             tomorrow on the Ben?'

'That part of me
I left in the French Quarter.
Also: a Poet with a white guitar,
who knows perhaps the whereabouts
of a Dual Blade – our Quest.'

               'Oh, *that*.
               She went doo-lally,
               not so much a breakdown as
               a case of over-revving.
               She got committed
               and I don't mean politics.
               But at that time she'd often mutter
               how a knife had got her number – '

'Think that's a quote – '

               'It is
               no state secret. Well you know
               how lyric poets exaggerate
               especially when they find themselves
               one sip short of the loving spoonful.'

'Yup, I mind
things got kinda tense at meal-times.
Is she
               incommunicado?'

               'Nah, she left the theatre years ago.'

'So,
          no visitors?'

16

'Not yet. I suggest
you pass a week in dreich Glencoe
where light is short but days are sweet.
Above 2,000 feet
                the ice is in good nick
and yer baldy-heided friend seems like
he'd front-point wi
the best. Yon saffron parka's
cool, I guess. Sherpa, is he?'

'Not exactly.
But – her?'

            'Stella? I suggest: ✉
            write her a letter.'

My Buddha had made himself at home
among the climbers of my youth,
MacBeth, Clackmannan, Shonagh, Slide,
had their table soon in roaring mood,
and as he drained the first pint of the night
this empty I
                (mere gutted vertical
                with flat cap and feet)
scribbled a letter to Stella
and some words of explanation, then we
hung out awhile, just marking place
like markers in a book, waiting

            to open

        on her reply.

SOME WORDS OF EXPLANATION

So what's I doing
in Glencoe with a Buddha
so brollied and heretical?
What's the Quest, pal?

                         Let's
                      b
                   a
                   c
                k

             t
           r
          a
        c
      k

   Let's say you woke alone,
bereft and empty as a sheath
whose blade is gone,
and your constituent parts
(body, head and heart)
have split up, scattered, gone to seed.

Naturally you are afraid.
But there's a sea inside your ear
and waves breaking upon that shore
and you hear
             a secret sharer.
Call it heaven-sent, call it Buddha,
call it your sole guide
through Debatable Lands.
And it says

   you are forfochen and forsaken
   you are empty
   you must find the Dual Blade
   round up the Company.

Now that's kinda cryptic
and you well might ask
where to start this Quest
and what's this Jewel Blade
when it's at home?
When you're at home the voice insists.

Some help, but all you're going to get.
So you rise and pack a bag
with toothbrush, slippers, penknife,
condoms, passport, change of clothes
and sling it in the deux chevaux
and GO.

Where?

Start with the heart,
last heard of climbing in Glencoe.

So here we are, still waiting for her letter.

STELLA WRITES FROM HOSPITAL

The sparrow teetering on the windy sill
raps, waits
   (I read your letter secretly)
till the woodworm crawl from the wood.
They shriek in very high voices,
stabbed by yon wee warbling bird
   (break my heart, no love in it)
that winks then flits
in the smug way of early birds.
Lucky atoms, that know no choices...

Some days just to wake and breathe
is murder, and I a sweet tormented Jain
must tip-toe through God's acres
hearing only screams –

   Dearie me. Today it seems
I woke without my second skin.

                *

Hours, days, weeks when the whole damn thing fits
   leaves in the gutter
      mesh completely,

Voices on the radio insist
   every little thing she writes
      is magic –

   Messages! Who'll do the messages for me
when something's moving in the trees
   and the stars are up against it

   and the arrangement of milk bottles
on the doorstep opposite
is the wrong arrangement

and a name ripples and is gone
   like a thrown stone
      in the depths of afternoon

        * * *

Three birds part the dawn
   and I lie counting
      creaks of the hospital gate,

noticing how absolutely
   everything is given
      in threes, these days

Numerology! (Mon pauvre Nerval
   it begins with coincidence
      that way madness wakes

   dresses in astrology
  rises to its feet
ends: hung by its tie

in the Rue de la Vieille Lanterne)

* * *

It is a healing blade.

The patient lies
on the crumpled bed of the North Atlantic.
On either side the surgeons stand.
Look East, look West –
they've nothing in their hands except
the very ordinary knives of death.
Nurse! Clear these clowns outa here,
their century is ending.
And my sweet, ailing country –

   I'm lyrical and raving. Here comes
my morning dose of Tedium.
These Protestants mean well, I know,
but their love's not blind so much as
as looking in the wrong direction.

A Journey, then? A Quest? Begin!
Come Thursday, I'll be stabilised by then.
(They've got me riding on 'mood elevators',
can you believe! Half the time
I'm singing on the penthouse ceiling,
next – croaking on the basement floor.
Think some fine tuning's still required.)

    The knife you seek
has parted from its sheath,
but that at least I'd recognise.
I lost it in some Asian yurt
when we split
back in the mid-Seventies
– that last long hectic trip!

I suggest: we try Tibet.

What the hell, it's big enough.

        *

    (It's called 'sampling')

I know a moor where bog myrtle blows
the veil aside, and on the sweet
clover of a machair beach
the slow beasts graze. Long waves retreat
around the giant Buddha of the coastline
stretched sleeping on the sand,
five withered continents   *R. Williamson, I think*
cradled in his hand.

    (An ancient craft, but seaworthy)

His dreams are so loud
I curl up in
these grainy blankets
and sift into his ear...

Rescue me, friends,
for only I can take you there,
and I'm told
that in his other hand he holds –

You got it.

*(New bolts, new portholes, new designs – but check
the underlying timbers: the old shipwrights' mark...)*

It is a healing blade.
State of the heart, archaic,
articulate, serrated,
blade of the future
    and the past reversible,
    drawn back across the scar
    requires no sutures
    but heals division and leaves skin
smooth as a baby's tum
and where its glittering edges meet
all divisions source and cease
and on that point
    someday we three
        will ~~dance~~   *stand*
            as
                one.

* * *

(Also known as 'sequencing')

Come early,
            come alone,
                        fuss not.

Bring mannish clothes for me
        and thistles from Brownsbank   *'The Wasted Man'*
            and roses from the Bostonian's garden

        so I may leave, when we escape,
        flowers that have no messages
but – prickly – love.

These tapes I've spliced

    This ain't no party
        This ain't no disco
            This is Western Swing

    Play a sang for me, Mr Shantyman,   *Shantih, man,*

    Western stars light up the sky –
        Ane doolie sessoun to ane cairfull dyte –
        And so sweet Jane, approximately –

These tapes I've spliced against the night.

* * *

Yup, it's called sampling,
patching a new voice
from all the old voices
rent in your throat.

    When I was a girl I had a rag doll
    but nane shall ken whaur she is gane

                       doo ee doo ahh

But this is not an elegy
and I amna tired sae much as
halfways crazy.   *The Drunk Land'*
I been to the Darklands to talk in rhyme.

    Whaur shall we gang
    and dine the day-oh?

                  dum diddy dum diddy doo

Out, out, out! That's a
cry not a quote –

    faithful as that rag doll

        Love
         Stella

(or otherwise, don't)

                Well press my pedal: wah wah wah

     *

A letter like that! She doesn't know –

Pack your sack, son,
we're leaving Glencoe.
Oh, and bring my brolly
to bend: those bars.

No comment further?

Nope. She wrote
the poem is not a Sunday paper
and this is not an Elegy
and the sickness of our days
is in an over-
dose of information
and the unnecessary
prescription of opinion.

Shake hands all round,
wipe clean our slate and go!

Goonight sweet youth of the Clachaig,
the snow banks gasp as we flash past.

*('And when the Buddha sat in his Immovable Spot below
the Trees of Enlightenment, he was approached by the creator
of the World Illusion...')*

The Axe-Man wakes, looks rough,
forjeskit, wabbit –
fuckt in baith languages.
   (Wha called him?)

Charred sodden leathers,
white-like aboot the gills,
he is something unspeakable
ben the city dump.

No just tae gallus,
bleak as Blantyre,
body back to blubber
the former Lizard King.

Ach, surely last night
was an incendiary device!
which could explain
this morning's ashy mouth.

(To rock, or no tae rock,
nae ither question...)

But last night he was
– incandescent! Was it
a gig, a rammie, a new
ice-route carved up the Ben?

He can't remember, canni
mind, doesni care to mind.
His bones ache. Wha calls him?
Wha cries him *Brock*?

(No other question
posed each dreich morn)

He feels akin
to the broken spring
of this knackered mattress
piercing his side.

From the depths of scuffed leather
he grasps an old penknife,
A Present Frae Ayr,
scrapes into rust, finds –

hard bright metal underneath!

Brock on the mattress
in the smouldering dump
under a grey and relentlessly
predestinated sky

laughs
and lights
the first of the day.
'Ach, Daith – ower blate tae dance wi me?'

Man of Earth,
son of the Earth-shaker,
    bleeding bull and rolling thunder,
mortal rock 'n' roller,

    rocking Earth's diurnal course,
rolling the stones and trees,
    needle-tormented Orpheus
wi torn leather knees –

'*FAUGGHHH!*
              Je me lance vers la gloire, pal!'

He rolls to his feet   and Up   and Out.

            (*'...and the mighty earth thundered with a hundred,
a thousand, a hundred thousand voices, declaring 'I bear you
witness!'. And the demon fled.'*)

                    Bud rose:
                There are other ways than purity.
                Our power's in the flow
                between the light side and the dark.

                Excise it with prayer and discipline?
                You might as well fillet the fish
                then ask it to swim...

STELLA, ESCAPING

... And so I left the hospital, sliding
through bent bars, dropping
lightly to the ground, brushing
lowly by sodden trees.

Sonics, optics, motion in full flow,
in pyjamas and carpet slippers,
I follow these odd friends
through a world that may never
conspire again, nor sing
my praises.

In one's right mind,
few ways to hide.
Mist and sober love
are all that cover me...

And, friends, there is so much of it!

– Stell, what brought on that breakdown?
(I enquired as she shook and shivered.)

'Some took advantage of my youth
and then again
my youth took advantage of me.'

– And left bad heart and broken language?

'Logorrhoea, pal. I crucified the swine
in forty-seven Villanelles. By then
even the milk bottles were talking.'

   She shook her head, accepted
the travelling rug Brud passed her
and bent beneath his brolly lit
with shaking hand the first in months,
drew deep   and blew
                        three perfect zeroes.

– Um, Stell...
Just how old are you?

'Twenty-five,' she said and laughed.
Then, punching her fist through the rings
added, 'centuries'
and climbed into the 2CV.

    Now narrative accelerates
jerkily as the Buddha takes the wheel
spinning lightly through his hands
and like with the stagecoach's
whirring spokes we glimpse
apparent stillness in that blur...

– Have faith, dear passenger!
We're bound soon
    to overtake
        another of the company...

CUT TO

    Brock's pushing his luck
as you or I might push a pun
to the limit. 'Ach,
that's what it's for,'
says he, stroking the gleaming
dropped cadence of the handlebars.

A chancy man! Loosen the clench
and the fist vanishes: that's him.
He's shorn his locks wi flint,
close to the skull and dangerous.

    I knew him once
    years back when he was mega
    but this world's no longer fit
    for guitar heroes
    any more than dinosaurs

(whom they curiously ressembled
in brain power and leathery skin
as they thundered on the stage
through steam and primal grandeur)
    and I grieve to see one arm awry,
    one leg shorter than the other
    and I guess he's trying to adapt
    or find some spot to die.

He shivers, coughs.
Either way:
        Mad Max he ain't.

But he's on the move,
his emblematic transport
British made, a burnt-out Norton.
He's pushed it till he's made his point,
now ditches it, limps on alone
with his sole instrument
the fretless bass Raw Power –

I hear him whistle as he leans into the wind,
forcing the way open like a stubborn door.

            – His destination?

Oh, very well –
          Nepal.
   Through the monsoon
he runs a voodoo rave
in down-town Katmundu:
hard-core groove.
Crag-rats & Goths hang out there
with Sherpas, cops, and double-dealers –
if you want to blend,
the colour's black and silver.
You can find him directly
on page 39.

        – Is that not cheating?

Maybe you'll miss something
in the intervening   voice.

           – I hae ma doots.

Your choice.

MEANWHILE A CURE FOR LONELINESS

There is a cure for loneliness
It's in the voices that keep company
your place after midnight

Here's another
Friend and cure –

Close
Your
Eyes

Let your attention travel
guided through the body
starting at the big toes
creeping through the litle toes,
ankle, shin, tibia, fibia
and so on up to the Head Office
where the Colonel sits scheming how to
make friends   unite the kingdom
and organise this world so well
and think so positively
he'll never ever have to die

Knock on that door
You might bring him to his senses
but don't count on it

As the Night Watchman clicks his flashlight,
follow him through the subway tunnels,
sewers, drains, arteries, veins,
lines of power and communications,
cellars, pumps and nervous systems...

Stick
With the
Night Watchman

through the night hours as
he does his rounds
and this body no longer belongs
to anyone especially
any more than a city can
and the city seems to stretch for ever
the whole city beneath the city
servicing the city
    beneath the skin

Already the body
seems large as Scotland
sprawled on the seas without sleep
    the abdominal lowlands rising and falling
    the mountainous chest expanding and contracting
    the north and western fingers
    trailing the waters
inhaling and exhaling
from one ice age to another

Containing so many
    making such journeys
    drawing such dreams
    to no sure conclusion
while your country is snoring
and we are still reiving
the Debatable Lands
    you might well wonder
    where light is breaking
    and if you can put it
together again

        But one thing's for sure
        you ain't lonely

                    Now
                    Open
                    Your
                    Eyes

A THIRD AND FINAL INTRODUCTION

Whether you woke to find yourself
An empty sheath
Or merely an insomaniac
In dire need of information –

Now you're being *filled in*
And one or two things
Are pressing where
You might suppose your heart to be

Now meet another of the company
We call him Grimpeur
Or sometimes Ken
Because he knows so much

Or used to till he deconstructed
And now he finds it hard to say
Just what it is he's saying
As he assembles in his room

And wonders why he had his breakfast
Among a crowd of Cambridge swans
Or maybe dons oh what's the differ
They all take off so slow

Out on the grapevine
(Curling round mullioned windows)
Sour grapes murmur
It's time to drink the wine

Rumours of a final expedition
With his old travelling companions...
But meaning endlessly receedes,
'It's fin de siècle, Jack – no Quests left'

He paces in his room until
he's ready to transmit
and as he clasps androgynous fingers
the fax is primed with his libretto:

let's see what's coming through –

'I am the passionate clinician, drawn
to snakes and sources, the tiniest
blue butterfly of a stranger thought.
That is, I've not concluded yet
my Notes towards an Introduction
to an Outline of Ecology of Mind –
sorry, but singing down below. Can't come.

Philosophy, it's rough these days.
Pay's terrible and meaning dissolves,
ungraspable as tenure –
words are castles in the air,
no foundations anywhere
except Guggenheim and Rockefeller.
Fame's itchy as these bites.

The dark interior when we close our eyes!
Excuse this scrawl –
                    It comes tonight.
No rendezvous but drums inside
say we'll rush to highest ground.
Now I am waiting by the watering hole
where all the passions come to die.'

– Well I think we can safely
put this one on hold,
(said Stella as she put up her hair
and accentuated the Gothic round her eyes
in preparation for our journey East)
though I did like that 'blue butterfly'.
It's all a bit beyond our Ken.

   Leave on the fax machine,
the Budder murmured.
*We'll catch him later. He's made
his passion his career –*
                    big mistake,
not necessarily fatal.
*To find the second of the Company
let's just turn softly
the next page
and be*

At the Up and Down Disco, Kathmundu

35

PART II   At the Up & Down Disco, Kathmundu

Praises of Desire – a remarkably obscene sonnet? – into the Voodoo
– a damned good laasi – Great Sex – conversations on a flying
carpet – backwaters of the Cam – it's quicker by phone – Come
Together

Namaste!

The beers went down like rivers of cold
as all except the Buddha dined
on yak-burgers & dall
till we were sold on
the party-party
at the Up & Down Disco –
                         Western Swing
was played that night and every night
beneath a starry voodoo; we stumbled
hooded & jazzed through the soft dark
streets of Kathmundu.
                         Fresh off the white slopes
I had a diamond ear-stud and a doubtful mind
but with Bud and Stella at my side,
felt ripe to sing the praises of Desire.

   'Desire,' I hicc'd, 'gets things done,
gets the book writ, the bairns born,
      tugs us up the big hill,
      and what but longing brings us back
to base when all else fails?

Ah folks! Tonight
      we tread the dancing floor
that birls through space below
      its ain wee glittering star,
and what's the rustling the radio
astronomer receives across the universe
but the swishing skirts of them
      who first came here to dance?
Shall I take issue with those powers?

              – In high places, friends,
as we traversed in from Europe
by way of Baltistan
and a couple of unnamed peaks before
descending the Lamjura
              we pushed the boat out...

     Now it has drifted back to hand
     laden with spices,
the lovely and the normal
redeemed again...'

And though I haivered
Stell smiled to that 'soft angora night'
and in my ear murmured:

     'What language quickens our page?
     Desire & Fear – that dual blade
     striking upward to the heart.
Though there be scars
     I love it
and tonight I'm up for –

              EVERYTHING!'

Yeah yeah yeah, the Buddha said,
hitched his bags a little higher, ad-
                              justed
the nifty trim of his Panama –

Desire is our condition, it is as mud
to the glorious paddyfields of Lower Nepal.
Pleasure converges on wisdom
like the sky onto the land.
          That is: apparently.

     'Then let us praise appearances
that give us excitations.
Your Auld Man had the truth of it
but it wasn't exactly exciting and
excitement's part of the True.
     Now let's gaun tae the birlin!'

Let these truths grow, he grinned.
But mind this, loon –
just because you like *something*
(love, truth, these carpets, the hashish
vivid faces offer us in the dark)
don't mean you have to buy *it.*
     That may be the only bum
note within your Western Swing –
your desire to perpetuate these nymphs
of happiness: they must hatch and fly.

If you want a good time
– hello, sailor! –
let the good time have you.

As I fumbled for rupees
and Stella wrote in lipstick
a quite remarkably obscene
sonnet on the Brit Embassy grille,
the Buddha clicked his heels, saluted
the low-down moon:

     Such is my heresy: I come
to accentuate and stress
the way things are,
     the haill clanjammfrie,
the rhythm pulsing through the blues
inside this auld receiver.
This is another Way, to say
that this is life and life is sweet,
and hurts, and ends, and then –

Ah well,
KJ had the right of it, it seems:
'let us pass out praises, bash the tambourine'!

We paid our dues & went into the voodoo.

INSIDE THE VOODOO

Je n'ai pas demandé cette musique
H.B. yelled, for it was LOUD.
A Norton roared up in the rafters
where my old pal Axe-Man gave it laldy –
'Hey, Axe!' –
and though his face was
seamed & hackit
           like his legendary jacket,
his sweat still blew some fuses
where he rioted as Dionysus –

   'Fuck me, it's da Poet!
   Long time no write!
   Aye kent you were a lassie.'

   White-faced Stella swarmed the ladder,
kicked in the headlight of his Norton,
   tugged his manky mane
and stared him out:
            'Amazin Grease!'
she hissed. 'Send me your hairdresser's name,
gut-bucket, so's I can send him a wreath.'

   'Ya wee blurb-merchant –
   if ya don't like the skulls,
   stay oota ma scullery!!'

    Aye, the light horse and the dark,
    how close they crop together
    the same grass. And how they falter
    when they're apart.

    Get me a drink without ceremony,
    say banana laasi laced
    wi Kukri rum. I havenae had
    yon bevvi for a thousand years.

    And loosen up, for Heaven's sake –
    tight ass-holes do not a Boddhisatva make.

At the bar I looked around,
partook of the endless endeavour of my kind
to get my shout in
while Brock and Stella grappled in the ceiling:

      Aye, complex jive & snogging,
sliding
  down the walls,
    the human race
most human when it's racing.

  The very cones
     gyred
        in the speakers of Desire
as the band from East Kilbride
played 'A Million Rainy Days',
distorting the distortion into something dark
yet beautiful in its analysis –

    I wonder if
      that's the trick of it,
to thrash the serpent till it sheds its skin
and comes out shining and we grin
at the sheer bloody rightness of it all.
(Some days I can do it, some days...)

Like the band, I.
How do these groovers style themselves?

'Rockin Buddha & the Forty Thieves.'

Well, pinch me, he murmured.
It's gnarly but I like it.
Oh, and that's a

     damned good laasi.

Talking of which:
a beautiful climber fresh off Nuptse
North Wall – nice one, bonnie fechter –
direct as a clean-struck inclined pick,
seized my arm to the boom-boom.
'Lovely
to see you, Drew, save one
for me, but who's your friend,
has he done something
                    in Tibet?
Face fits, can't place the accent.'

'Somebody told me that his name was Bill.'

'Oh, do the ron-ron, dude!' she cried,
took my Buddha by the hand,
yanked him from his dwam.
'Maybe we met in Cham –
                    your face
minds me of times I thought I'd die
and I was unafraid yet keen to see
what   happened   NEXT!
So, great unknown – will you dance?'

Ah she was fresh & ardent as a blade
drawn, untipped, to the quivering
point of desire.
                    Bud hesitated –
that 3 months later she'd lie broken
across the icy knee of Gangapurna,
some suspected, but he knew.
Though the joints were jumping
    hand to mouth
and the Up & Down was
    hotter than a sweat lodge
and her incense mingled with a hint of yak
    and consequently
smelt like Heaven –
    still I shivered.

Pleasure, he said, *is a great good*
and if we waited till our dance was pure,
who would get off their arse?

'O pooh!' she said. 'But can you dance?'

Jings! he said, *I'm just a chancer*
who moves on lightly as a dancer
never ready for a partner
and all my words are wasted birds
compared to this.
                    Your beauty
strikes me dumb
surely as this boom-boom biffs me deaf.
Here, Drew, take my hat,
go calm your friends up in the rafters.

Now let's go shake, cutie-face.

Great sex, the Buddha said
when we met up again next morn,
a lil s l o w e d u p from the night's
high jinks at the Up & Down,
    sure is a flick
from the tasselled edge
of the carpets of Paradise.
    I see
 (glancing at Axe subdued
strumming in the corner of Teshering's
glory hole, climbers' heaven in downtown Kat
where we'd been idly doing deals
in second-hand carpets and sharks' eggs
left by Japanese expeditions,
whilst nibbling glances from
that witty Sherpani's almond eyes),
I see the Body's with us once again.
Two out of three. Good egg!

'Wise guy, huh?'

 This time round
I am Bud wiser. Heh,
gather round, bairns,
for in this hand I'm holding
a traditional Truth:
   the Futility of Desire.
In the other – the heretical
   Truth of its beauty.
Holding out his fists:
So what's it gonna be today –
wisdom, or the other?

Poet sighed and tapped one fist
but we never knew which she'd chosen
for when Bud spread his palm, we were air-
borne in the cool air over Katmundu...

...Yup, I assure you, out at sea
dolphins smile to hear
    sexual pleasure has lately been re-born
mutual, free of fear and domination.

'Bud, you assure us of some very strange things.'

Heh heh, I like to keep you guessing
    so's you don't completely trust
your secret sharer. Still
    unlike you former Christians,

Muslims hold sexual pleasure a fore-
taste of the Paradise you may inherit
should you invest the spirit well.
    Sex! A shining hook
            let down from above

– just don't get hung up on it.

'Christ let me doon gently
(the Axe-man moaned, clutching
the edge of our aerial tapis)
        I'm no just so happy
when I canni touch the groon.'

        Play us a tune, my earth-bound friend,
    for we are Nine Miles High.
How neat the kingdoms of the Earth unroll
    those reds, them blues, the huge
            Saharan yellow!

                Axe
    strummed Raw Power
and through the pain of his arthritic fingers
    plucked an anthem of those heady days,

            ♫   *If Wishes Were Fishes,*
                Would Men Would Swim Free? ♫

and we ourselves could not stop laughing
as we rocked the fantasy, sublime,
ridiculous as sex itself, or this
        flying carpet zooming West...

    'O those hours upon the carpet'
(Poet murmured as she
took off her socks and looked down),
    'the hours we unroll when making love.'
She flicked a comb through her chopped hair
then levelled it at me:
        'Want to pull – or shove?'

Something stirred in my chest, turned over once
like a wee beastie in its lang winter sleep...

I gripped her comb, raked it
slowly through my uplifted hair
felt the teeth grip
and knew that I could never
pass this way again
nor hold a woman as before
now I knew in all embraces
I'd strained only
to *become her...*

        'Take it easy, huh?'
    she said. 'Boy, do I remember
all the patterns from way back,
        the fingers' calligraphy tracing
            the thousand names of Desire
all over our bodies
        with particular emphasis
            descending around the eyes...
                Heh heh, you do look queer.'

        Remember chum,
    the lotus is only
        a tearless variation
    on the onion.

    So greit if you must.

45

'We're
         coming
                down.

        Bud, where we headin?'

       This carpet's going home. Morocco.
        Back to its maker, among the Berbers
of the High Atlas. I suggest
        you look there
                on the next stage of your quest.
To find your Blade
you first must earn the Sheath.
Could be
            when you've suffered some
I'll meet you there
            in the next section.

    'But but but – !'

        – But first I'll
         drop
             you
                off
in Cambridge, for you've still to find
the last of the company:
                    Ken, the mind.
Without some critical
intelligence you'll never grip
the jewelled blade, let alone
hang on to it.
            For a while
you're on your own –

or, as the wife said before
she turned to a pillar of salt,
        that's your lot, chum.

BYEEE!

The carpet tipped
   over green fields
      and clutching each other w
                   e
                  f
                   e
                    l
                    l

headlong into the backwater of the Cam.

The backwater of the Cam

Just a bittie sodden
and squeezing out slime,
at the porter's box
we were handed a note
from our old compadre:

    <u>Today's antinomies</u>

    Water is wet   Appearing
    Sky holds up birds   Disappearing
    Earth under our feet   In the vast
    Solid solid solid   Spaces of Mind

        videlicit un 2cv –

– 'Ding doon the door, lads!'
  Stella cried. 'Without us
  the thinker's flipped
  and only he knows where our blade is.'

We broke in, the room was bare,
the only books: *Appearance & Reality*
in the Works of T.S.Eliot by
F.H. Bradley –
    and a *BT Directory*.
No clues, no forwarding address.
We'd lost our mind. Without him
we'd forgotten all the rest.

And I was incomplete in all things now
        what with the world
born of its onrush
into oblivion   and the dark
scorch mark in my heart
where she'd
        passed right through me
at close range –

   Sure it won't kill you,
and there's always some way to get home,
but some things don't come
your way twice, and one absence
is one too many
        when Homo Scotorum
comes home late one time too often
and sticks a pizza in the microwave.

...Nights under the desk spotlight when
  loneliness that tightrope stretches
  such distances no phone lines cross
  and spirit yes that word is called for
  though we dislike its spangly tights
  sets out to put one foot before
  gripping a tremmelin pole
  talking to itself I mean to anyone
  waiting on the dark far side...

     'WAKE UP!'
        (Poet shouted,
   picking up BT's blockbuster),
'This has gotta be a Clue, for here
we have – The Wrong Directory!'

   'Uh, would ye put that
intae ma ear
a wee bit less succinctly?'

   'Certainly, Axe,' she replied.
'Your sonsie face wi puzzlement
is seamed and hackit
like your legendary jacket,
witness to a thousand crashes – '

'Stella, ye've a mooth
I could post a haddock in.'

'If you don't like the kitsch,
stay outa ma kitchen.
A telephone directory of Dublin
when it oughta be of Cambridge,
is surely a hint –
                    I bet
we'll find his name in here
and he's moved his Chair
to the Universe City there.'

And as she spoke
         the said Directory
flipped open at K.

So has the Poet (I enquired) become
merely a good guesser, or
a Master of Reality
in her crack-up years?

'No, but I am no longer
the Slave of Illusion'
                    (the scene-setter murmured
as she ran her finger down the line)
– 'No verbs! No qualifying phrases!
An ultimate minimalism, such as we see
in the very very short stories on tombstones.

    GOT IT!'

I dialled the numero   ☎
and *there we were.*

Dublin: it's quicker by phone

'Phone service has come long way
fae ma day' the cocky muscle man
murmured as we trudged that fair city.
'Look! A spire!'

'Is that an uplifting slogan
or a piece of architecture?'

'Aw, push aff or I'll smite ye.'

But the duo turned the corner
and they were trinity,
for there was the Quad
and in it a tree
and beneath it,
disputing with Bishop Berkeley,
G.
   (Ken)

**The shards of my psyche
are come together again.**

* * *

INTERMISSION

The night is nearly over
(however long it's been)
though the day's not yet begun

An *Intermission* comes to mind
Twitch back the curtain
– a lengthening slash
glinting like a razor
severing sky from earth

Easy to see
these nights are needed
when they're nearly over

and half the virtue of the Quest
is rounding up the Company

*

'Understanding may well be
universal' (Ken murmurs
as he packs his books for
the next stage of our journey)
'– but hope is local
                    thrawn
                        specific

and keeps returning for no good reason
inappropriate
                    unbidden
like a brickie bent whistling under his hod

or the seeding thistles
such as rise, swathed in poppies, by Pittenweem Road'

                                        (*To*
                                        Be
                                        Continued

as they must)   ·

PART III Travails in the High Atlas

To resume the resumé – Into the Drylands – tourists and terrorists – Kenny Dalgleish – meeting the Hadji – comparing notes on Black Houses – cheap labour and Stella's stanza – A Carry-out Episode? – days of sweat and succour – A Munelicht Flittin – a graduation surprise – one star awake

TO RESUME THE RESUMÉ

We
have all gone
into the drylands
for days, months, years –
hard to say how long
your life's been wrong.
Such time is measured by
new nicks around your eyes.

Times
when I for one
felt myself a jug
   (broken in three
   by a single parting blow)
forever run dry...

   (like that woman who, when I asked
   why she drank so, replied
   'I live in mortal fear of dehydration'

and, later,

   'I'd have drowned myself years ago
   but for my parents,
   their feelings, ya know'

and when she kissed me at the Christmas party
sitting among dead needles under the tree
her thirst was terrible
and we swayed to her place
each hoping the other had the bottle

– 'I wake up each morning,
   trying to forgive myself' –

and the streets of Edinburgh
were white and not in order
and on the windscreen a human finger
had written   PEECE – GOD LUVS YOU
and it went under our defences
and she began to weep...

That woman with the hair
colour of bracken in late autumn,
sleeps alone and reads thrillers
much of the night   waiting
for the world
to confirm her suspicions

   'And after all, what's positive thinking
   but a sustained effort to kid yourself? And who
   can really afford to go south in winter?'

This little late night reading
     is for her
        among others

for how could I forget
        not recognise
            or fail to love

my own and braver sister?)

INTO THE DRYLANDS

'Dust on our bags and our capes'
Nose clogged, throat choked,
couldn't speak
               fair to any man:
'All bloody buggers round this place'

Once under midday sun
a golden wheel
whirred by without stopping.

Days without shade
nights without stars
even our mule
                 avoided us.

Sure it was a dry
and flegsome world
and much rougher than littoral
the sand in our shoes.

They say poets sing.
There's a lotta loose talk.
I've seldom met one
could even whistle 'Three Blind Mice'.

Sing?
             Guess I came near to croaking,
there.

*

   Dawn – cold – we stumbled through
a fault in the desert, scunnered,
dumfounert, forjeskit, boots shot,
lips split,
               our stubborn mule
the only optimist left (H.B.
was long gone, 'less it were he)
as we slid and clattered
down that gully...

But halfway in, the ravine shrugged
or the mule kinda changed its mind
the way history does once in a while:

    a slash across the hillside
    glittered like a blade
    below it everything

        bled

    Green

The mule shucked our baggage and ran.

*

Five faces, four human, one
more or less,
nose down in that water.

Drank. Threw up. Drank more.
Lay belly-down by cool waters.

    '*Une source,*' Ken murmured,
    'sprung straight from the dust,
    doubtless a glacier-melt
    sent down to us
            by higher powers.
    Heh heh! This dawn is not my enemy's.'

Water in our eyes, ears, hair,
we stared at the terraces below
stacked like plates, each
with its garnish:
almond in blossom, olives, figs,
and the morning breeze
like a perfect waiter
            shimmied up
to ask what we most wanted...

    Between aridity and life
        runs a slash
    the width of an irrigation channel –

      miracle, for sure
but one honed by human hands.

'Juxta
         position,'
    said Stella as she
rinsed her hair from red to fair,
knocked out her hat and spat, 'the whole
    armature of experience, the motor
    of modern art.
              If I had a hammer
I'd knock up a sestina.'

'No, no!' they cried.
    She lay back, cracked her pursed lips,
        began to whistle.

'Sod that,' Brock said, lifted
the jewelled binoculars that hung
 from the neck of the mule:
    'Woodsmoke, a village, water-mills,
    five hours hence. Ya beauty!
                        – Let's roll.'

*

Up front she sang
'These Boots Are Made For Walking'.
Behind her, Kenny ducked and hummed   ♫
'Dark Isle' and 'The Flowers of the Forest'
She turned and looked at him
and between them flew something
like a pass
              so quick I couldn't tell
who now held the ball,

but something had been exchanged
and happiness was punted
way into the sky
where it hung for hours
descending slowly at dusk
as we entered the village.

              Oh catch and wrap it in your arms
                 and fold it quietly in your pack
                    like music for a better day –
                 then tomorrow back to the Drylands

TOURISTS AND TERRORISTS

Two men rose like quivers of heat
from the dried-up wadi, greeted us
in Allah's name, demanded a light.
We agree: God is good, shook on that.
But the tall man's grip
          tightened on my wrist
as he bent to light his cigarette
and the short one drew a knife
to pare his nails;
          in the glittering
I saw the three who stood behind us.

It's that simple: sun overhead,
four blades, the oddly plastic
barrel of a semi-automatic
stroked idly against the ribs.

I wondered how this was going to feel,
hoped it brief, especially for her
whose fair hair shivered in the heat
while the youngest plucked her necklace,
swung it gently in his hand...

'Well,' she said, 'no point
giving up smoking now. Can I
mooch one too, please?'

    '*Hal anta mai?*'

      'Whit's he sayin?'

    ' "Whose side are you on?" '

'Ooh la la,' Stell murmured. 'Such ancient questions.'

    '*Hal anta Americain?*'

'Je ne suis pas americain, nous sommes
des écossais. (Hold on tight, babe.)

Je n'ai pas fait cette guerre. (Christ,
we should've stayed at your cousin's,
the Archduke's.)'

> '*You speak very bad French. So,*
> *you are English, I think?*'

'Pas du tout!'

> '*Alors, British.*'

'Pas tellement. Scottish. Wee place up North.'

The youngest man looked up.
'*Scotland!*
> '*Scottishers?*
> > *Kenny Dalgleish!*'

'Oui, oui. Kent his faither. Uh,
j'ai connu son père...'

> '*Ours too is a small country,*
> *our football team also loses.*
> *One day we shall win, Inshallah.*'

'We are travellers, innocent travellers.'

> '*There are no innocent tourists.*
> *You must know this.*'
The blade lay on my cheek, scraped:
> '*You need a shave, mon cher,*
> *you look like a terrorist.*'

– He laughed, flipped the blade
high into the blue, where it spun
whittling the breeze to nothing,
    and when it clattered at our feet

        all men had gone

and we were alone in the wadi,
        sweat running from our boots.

'Think ah've wet masel.'

'Nice knife,' Ken noted, 'but not the one.'

'These bad dreams
should not be in poetry
but some days insert themselves
like a shiv between the ribs.'

We walked on, but from then
the world was hotter, focused,
as if those men had been
                              guardians
lounging at the arc of an invisible lens.

Up ahead, distance and almond trees.
We drank a little wine and came quickly to the village,
pausing only every so often to be sick.

MEETING THE HADJI

Three weeks into the High Atlas,
rising each day
further into debatable lands
where we could only guess the argument.
Hard light, harsh lands, honed faces
with manners more courteous than our own,
each with a knife
winking at the hip
and hospitality proportional to poverty
as is the way
with mountain people in this world
as though their scabby villages
are last undrowned outcrops
of an earlier and better world...

You won't like this thought,
but there was a war on
in a not so distant desert
and we wondered
whether chaos, like cruelty,
is a constant
that changes only its location
and so will always find a home.

I said you wouldn't like it.

We had gone *behind the war*
as though it were a curtain, a
            tapestry of violence,
and now
the heart draws it back,
            revealing –

– A mule clicked down the canyon.
On it an old and humble man
relaxed, radio cradled to his ear.

'Labesse! Becher! How goes the war?'

> *'As always. Did you meet my son*
> *at the souk — has he sold goats?*
> *These damn Yankee batteries, so dear...'*

We sheltered in the shadow of the reddish rocks.
The war went on through tiny speakers,
distorted, lost in that high stony place,
awful of course
                but not everything
for we had glimpsed the timeless village
and now shared oranges & cigarettes with him.

Dry smoke   sharp juice
all life was in   the alternation
desert war   rest in the mountains
head-splitting heat   cool under the rock
silent afternoon   sputtering radio
this orange   this cigarette
desire   the end of desire
this Berber   these Christians

> and like a knife from its sheath,
> like a foot from its boot,
> came a slight easing...

> *'Now tourists don't come to the city,*
> *the shops don't buy from us*
> *   and thus*
> *we can't buy feed for our dry season.*
> *Sheep and goats starve alike.*
> *Vous savez, tourists like some birds*
> *are signs of peace and settled weather.*
>
> *O send down clouds, Allah!*
> *If we can't have peace or tourism,*
> *let us at least have rain.*
>
> *And if you have no money, friends,*
> *then give us a song.*

We looked to Brock, he shook his head.
'Ma mind is on ma ain countrie,
where clouds like grizzlin bairns
cling to the mountain's side.'

Poet coughed and then
with unaccustomed shyness rose.
'An old lament,' she said then sang
in her husky thin high voice:

♫   Love in time brings dejection,
     We were drunk on projection,
     But now I'm quite sober,
     And I'm in my right mind –

     But I never loved no one
     Like I loved that someone
     And I saw this world most clearly
     When I was going blind...   ♫

She stopped and stooped a moment
under the red sky, bitter-sweet,
Heartbreak adjusting her sandal.

The Hadji clapped slowly, twice.
Though you have food, I see you're hungry.
You have water, yet you thirst.
I do not know your pilgrimage
but I invite you to follow
back to my village.'

He rose and touched his hand
first to his lips, then to his heart
and we in clumsy fashion responded.
He re-mounted and led us there,
poor, assured, a distant war
cradled to his ear.

'No,' we said gently, 'we do not want
to come and see you 'make the folklore',
no, nor take pictures of your daughters
miming prettily in the fields.
These travesties are painful, and must cease.'

'*Wakha*,' the old man grinned, stroked
his lang neb. 'Agreed.
So let's converse until the yellow rider
slips from the saddle of the sky.
(I am expected to speak this way,
don't let it charm or bother you.)'

We sat down by a broken wall
around a few untended trees
in thin dry grass like clumps of hair
clung to an aged skull.
'Peaceful here, we like it.'

'You've noticed, but are too polite to say.
The terraces of the old ones are crumbling.
In empty palmeries the water channels
return to sand.
                 Now nothing here
holds water long, the land returns
to slow mode, half asleep, unkempt
where once were dates and almonds,
saffron, olives, wheat gleaned by goats.'

Comparing notes on Black Houses

'My country too has empty hillsides,
old walls crumbling by the sea.'

'We did not call it "folklore" then.
We called it nothing but *our way*.
Our festivals were enacted
for no eyes but our own.
There was no talk of "the community".'

'My people were small tenant farmers
not much impressed
by anything but work and land.
What's left from their labours?
A way of standing,
                    photogenic air.
The land's a husk,
the grain's elsewhere.'

    'Doubtless their sons built cities
    or went abroad. Who does not want
    words on the T shirt
    and new blue jeans
    bought from the infidels he curses?'

'There was a cow, chickens, a bit land,
a boat dragged on the machair.
Their houses too were low and dark,
full of smoke, familiar
as fatigue and dignity. Doubtless
their eyes watered.'

    'My friend, you too have a peasant's mentality.
    I expect tourists came then from the South?'

'They did indeed. Left enchanted,
wrote books about it.'

    'Your women too are stubborn and short-legged,
    then flash a smile, making work worthwhile?'

'Don't let Stell hear you say that,
but: yes. They know their worth,
will not be messed with.'

    'Our sons retire from the grocery trade
    in France and Spain, build
    European villas beside the ancestral
    huddle of stones. I live in one
    with solar heating.
                It's very nice.
At night the heat-pipes whisper
my time is past.'

'Hard men, hard hands, hard minds,
softened only in their eighties
as they prepared to take their leave.
When I was young
                    we had two pear trees,
a garden like this one.
Grandfather the saddler gave me his penknife
and wrapped his huge old hands round mine
and taught me how to graft
new shoots to old trunks. Pear blossom
drifted on our shoulders as we talked.'

   'Your hands, broad and coarse as mine,
   could work leather or the fields.'

'I can take a hint. What needs done?'

   '*Shokaran*. This wall must be re-built
   against the goats. Also some hoe-ing,
   the highest channel shored again.
   May I allot your muscular friend,
   yourself, the technician, the unmarried woman,
   each to their suited task?
   Your patient mule
   can walk in circles, drawing water.

'Pal: you're on.'

* * *

(That pointy ball of happiness you caught
and snuck into your pack when you were searching:
long ways from home, and lost, and found again
together with a handshake and an honest trade
and eyes met for once across the barriers –
be close now as remembered hills,
the Alt a' Mhuilann, and Rest and Be Thankful.)

Cheap Labour

We spent the war in that high corrie
beyond all roads and radio,
worked long days for Hadji,
dossed down nights inside his byre,
worked hard, slept well,
content to shape another's garden.

'Sometimes salvation,
like a worthy ox,
cannot be yoked head-on'
the old man grinned.
'Anyway, you're cheap labour
while our young men are in the city
or baking bread on the plains of war.'

And Stella borrowed my penknife
to scratch above the old man's mantle

Sweat and sleep and in-between
smoke and watch the moon awhile
flattering the scraggy palms;
may channeled water flow each day,
and be clear discourse through your dreams.

A CARRY-OUT EPISODE

– So we're like beer bottles then,
(the Grimpeur sighed one night
as we dossed down in the byre),
No deposit, no return?

  None answered, Axe groaned,
  for we knew by Ken's tone
  that we were in for
      another fireside seminar
  of speculation from the thinker...

– Yet nights like this below the stars
(untwinkling at this altitude)
make me deal this wildcard
among the suits of possibility:
Bud may actually be right.

So, play it:

we're flittin
from incarnation to carnation
like dizzy bees
layin up honey sweet or sour –

in which case nothing is as it appears
in which case Western Man's
stoic premise and speedy ways
    are both completely fuckt
in which case the bodies we mourn and bury
    are empty shell-cases
    and the bullet's lodged elsewhere
in which case the people in the street
    have wings beating so fast we can't see 'em
in which case my cat Spike
    (let us consider my cat Spike)
    isn't a nimble machine for consuming Whiskas

In which case everything disappears but nothing ends
In which case we'd best mind what we chuck
    for it returns like a boomerang
    in this life or the next
    to get us in the neck
And Justice will be done
not by a Judge but by an impersonal
causal principle
    that can't be bribed or flattered
by even the most sleekit of cats
In which case everything is white
    as I saw it once on Princes Street
        all colours added by our eyes

In which case we're investigating a mystery
    the case is never closed

In which case this same flower that blooms today
    tomorrow will bloom again
    when death's another name for pollination...

    'Yeah yeah yeah!' Axe smashed a chord
    that rattled the termites in the Hadji's shed.
    'Jings, do I hate wishful thinking!
    Sure and the turtle people believe
    the universe rests
    on the back of a...
    guess what?...turtle.
    Sod it, we're all gonna die.'

Poet blew gently across the lip
of a bottle of so-called Pale Ale
and the sound dispersed among the ghostly
saffron fields that lay around us.
    'So what does the turtle rest on?' she enquired.

– According to the hottest theorists,
it's *turtles all the way down.*

We fell silent,
the last beer bottles clinked.
We had a cigarette, lit another
and stared into the night.

Deep dark secret river, on either side
ripe willows stir.
The night breeze drifts like solar winds,
bearing the invisible love-making of trees.

(Still worrying about those turtles.
I hope their shells are strong.)

DAYS OF SWEAT AND SUCCOUR

Brock took up the filthy oud
our gaffer handed him one night,
found it took his crippled fingers well.
Raw Power (mind yon fretless bass?)
lay wrapped in sacks, unplucked –
'Nae use tae man nor beast,
wi'oot youth nor electricity'.

Fast by an ingle, night by night
slowly he acquired
the trance-music of the *gnawa*
that can drive out devils
or drive insane.
                'Hey,
it's only ethnic radio,
but it seems to cool my crazies.'

Two Tuaregs appeared at dawn
across the boundary of the village,
near-black their faces,
piercing blue their robes.
One held a gimbri, the other
banged a drum. Nothing was said,
but they stared at Brock
who glared back,
but when they strode on up the mountain
he bowed his head, picked up the oud,
and with a sortof laugh
set off in pursuit...

He returned days later,
hirpling still, his left arm bent
mair than before,
but when he played thereafter
his fingers were quicker
and precise in their pressure
as acupuncture along the ear.

'Don't ask,' he said, 'just
dinni speir.'
                    And, later,
'Yon power's no skin-deep.
Nae need to be a loony teen nor leap
across a stage tae prove it!'

And Stella started to relax among the men,
and women walked a little taller where she passed,
and showed her how to grease her hair
and rim her pale blue eyes with kohl.
And Stella said
                    'All truth is good news
                    however dark it seems'
And, later,
                    'Happiness
                    is not my happiness'
And she wrote less
but her hands were steady.

Ken's hands grew harder as he worked
salvaging the basic
clapped-out machinery – but his mind
moved less like metal, more like water.
        'Wittgenstein was an engineer
        who loved to help things come unstuck
        and start to work, men's minds for one.'

He said
            'The world is everything
            outside the text. Man,
            it's so mean to always *mean*.'

And, after a long day sharing
the two-man saw among the pines,
            'As a working hypothesis
            it's not entirely ridiculous
            to act as if another exists.'

He became
                a favourite of the children
for they found him
not entirely ridiculous
and he could make things disappear
and re-appear,
and tie the
most complex knots that pulled
free with one tug
on the end produced from his ear.

A MUNELICHT FLITTIN

(run through the MacDiarmidtron)

It wis the dowp
o a dreich an dowie day
that left us dead choked
                all shagged oot.

Night, and the drizzle swayed away
like someone had turned a watering
can elsewhere. The moon rose
bloody and pink, Axe
coaxed a fire behind some rocks.

We unwrapped our bedrolls in a Pictish ring.
Ken cut a root, whittled a whistle
to play 'The Northern Lights'
very badly
as at best of times it is,
while Stella hunched and fed the fire
with myrtle leaves, to sweeten her thoughts
when the world smelled bitter.

'Why do we linger here,'
she said, 'so far from home?
Does anyone see us
in their mind's eye at all?'

Brock shook his head, bent lower
upon his oud, scrunching
Django music from those strings.
Ken heard his faither's language rise
through years of university training
through sedementary layers of reading,
travelling, Rock 'n' Roll, oh millions of words
like tiny dead animals made chalk –
like the outcrops around us
that hard linguistic core persisted
strangely in the moonlight
when softer things had worn away.

   – A munelicht flittin, he breathed,
and his speculation emerged
in his faither's leid:

Can onybody see us? I hae ma doots.
Gin there be a God,
     yon great een canna keek through
     sae sma a crack in time as oors
tae spy whit's gaun doon here!

Yon Absolute is tae lang sichtit,
and oor warld's tae nearby
     for his kennin – believe me,
we graipple here wi dreids and fairlies
he canna even see.

He canna scale doon, and like a giant
peerin in the weans' gang-hoose,
     he's shuttit oot. He canna warm hisel inby,
     an mutterin *The bairns are raised the nicht*,
hirples aff across the galaxy.

Yon stairvit yearnin in the blaw
when ye look into the lift at nicht
     aiblins it's no you but grievin herts
     o wheechin angels wha canna slow
eneuch tae enter this airt.

We're on oor tod, or micht as well be.
Above us, shootin stars stravaig,
   the mune's a pale rider wha canna dismount.
   Whit the hell, my faither would say –
It's whit ye dae when naebody's lookin that counts.

– Ken folded his penknife.
'I've been a wanderer aa my life   ♫
and mony's the sicht I've seen'
he sang then mercifully
lobbed the whistle into the fire,
turned in for the night.

   And I
lay staring at emerging stars,
strung as I was among my Company
wha tugged my brain this way and that,
as I tried to dree my weird.
Ken's speculation though irrefutable
(and maistly in soond Scots)
had left me low and feart...

   Till Axe winked and strummed
another number on his oud:

♫   But aa this doesni alter
     The orbit of Jupiter,
     Nor bring the sodger hame frae the Front.

     And if the sodger laid doun his arms,
     Said 'Sod this for a gemme o toolies',
     This would not alter the orbit of Mars.

     An if it did, the planets are jist
     Marbles pinged roun the playgroun o nicht
     For ane saison, then back in the pouch.

     Ach, yer brain's nippit but
     Ony thocht's at best is jist
     A fine example o a thocht.

     An atom's big as ony star
     And we as sma as it,
     So hit me E major, kid –

     An hit it hard.

Wan...twa...three...fower:

The Earth's a bride
in the gounie that her mama wore,
    She was just 17
    billion years old,
                so,
    how could I dance wi another
    syne I saw her birlin there?

An aa the bricht stars were her dowrie...' ♫

*

A GRADUATION AND A SURPRISE

The young men came home.
The war was over
or rather   moved elsewhere
and we were fit   but surplus.

Our last task:
clearing the village's main well.
Brock abseiled down
and many muffled curses came back up
till finally he surfaced
covered in gunge. He silently
gave Hadji
an ancient sack that clunked,
then plodded off to wash.
The bucket went down,
came up clear.
           'Well done,'
Hadji said quietly, 'and now
it's time to say farewell.
You have connected East to West
with honest sweat, now you must go
back to your people. But first
come to the square for a feast tonight.'

We washed, changed to travelling clothes,
and walked under stars
we'd never see so clear again
to the meeting place among the palms.
At the centre of the silent crowd,
some holding candles, the Hadji sat
cross-legged on an oddly
familiar carpet,
and at his knees
a filthy sack and crusted sheath
that flames, reflected, seemed to eat.
The old man looked at us and grinned.

'That carpet – '
You flew it once.
'And this sheath?'

The one you seek. Tibetan.
You observe this curious motif

You find it also carved
on Celtic crosses
on your side of the world.
Take it: it's yours.

Ken stepped forward,
wiped the sheath upon his sleeve,
turned it slowly in his hand,
and candlelight etched his high cheeks
as he stared into that ancient pattern.

'I see,' he said at last. 'I see.
The inevitable still surprises.
Bud, I declare you've aged,
or else a master of disguises.'

This wearing century
has finally caught up with me.
Look around at your companions:
even archetypes must age.
   You once knew me as 'The Bear'
(way back, when Poet was a man
and we were climbers, of a sort,
dossing round the Himalaya.)

'What's a name but thistledown'
said Ken
'a very floating signifier?'

      'For sure,' Brock muttered,
      'a thistle by any other name
      is still a prick, huh, Zen?'

   Poet drew a shawl across her face.
There were mineshafts in her heart
sealed off for her own good
and she would never descend
those ways again.

   'Aye well,' she said at last,
   'if you don't like the duel,
   don't chase the jewelry, boys.'

   The Hadji, H.B., clapped his hands
and the farewell feast began.
We smoked and shot the breeze till dawn,
much singing, Brock played
most furious for the dancers,
great bull-shit among the ox-turds,
firelight rising, and a touch of opium
sticky on our words until
the worlds began to slide again
the carpet's edges gleamed
the first cock stirred
and we were
in for

Brock kept the oud but
wrapped his ancient leather jacket
round the wildest child there.

The Immam gave Ken a chasèd leather belt
slipped through the loop of the sheath,
buckled tight. 'Don't lose this again.'

Stella hummed and coughed
as though about to make a speech
but only held her palm out to the people
then slowly placed it on her heart
and turned away

and we left that village
one star awake

In Marrakech – the Djemma el Fna – a debate on Karma – Axe-man's answer – Stella and the Monkey-man – who by fire – on the bus to the coast – Interlude in Essaouira – Fear not

In the Djemma el Fna

All narratives are narratives of desire
and the souks of Marrakech
are a pre-Modern maze.
We stepped down from the carpet
and I sensed again like
scent through urgent stench
the possibility of happiness.
Perhaps my blade was here...

I did not request this music,
said HB, lithely body-swerving
trance-drummers of the medina
who drift impervious through the preaching
herbalists and hustlers of the Djemma el Fna –
– nor do I question it.
Here people like portunate days appear
to shower gifts upon you
                    but remember –

    – 'There's nae such thing
       as a free bangle,'
       Brock grunted, shaking off the gleaming cuffs
       young ladies hung upon him.

Just so.
And all I ask from you, mes belles,
is a serious price. Thank you.
And another for M'selle.

    'Sometimes a bangle is only a bangle,
    not more karma going down?'

No, but it's pretty
and the price is fair,
and they need the money
and a little courtesy glows
like lemons on the underside of leaves.

We went through the souks,
not knowing the language used
   our eyes
and read each moment of exchange
   as fair deals, fear or avarice
written on faces in secret ink
   that registers then vanishes.
We followed the pickpocket
   to see him deftly even up
some local inequalities
   and in an alley pay off the police.

You see rip-offs great and small,
the rich cheat
and the poor fail,
but I would ask you to remember
the invisible adjustments
               of karma,
that internal market no one beats.

A debate on karma

'I hate that karmic shite,'
Axe muttered, testing a gimbri.
'It's one fer the money,
twa fer the money, three
fer the money in this warld.
An gin the human brew is wersh,
don't sweeten it wi honey.
Cash is the sultan's dawg
aye returning to its maister.
Some get whit they deserve,
   maist dinni. End o sad story.'

No, end of sad episode.
There's more
                lives overleaf.
I know, I've been there.

        'But *we* don't know that' – Ken objected –
        'All we see is the lemon grow,
        be plucked, squeezed, discarded.
        100 pages, 100 lives – may be,
        but little use to little me,
        when I can't remember none of it.'

The Buddha looked a bit...embarrassed.
Cracked a nut, scratched his cheek,
muttered he'd been up late last week,
in any case was out of practice
debating with mortals, claimed he
would tell us if he could (winked),
but he had promises to keep...
Put his hands in his pockets,
felt with his thumb,
and sighed.

        Ah, Ken,
    in that case
    all I see is bitter
    and there can be no peace,
    no justice and no remedy.
    You might as well go home,
    bolt the doors, fix a stiff
    gin, slice the lemon and
    your life alike, and stick
    the future in the microwave
    along with what remains
    of your horror-laden century.
    Stick your head in while you're at it.

We stood dismayed,
and Bud seemed old and far from home.
as I put my arm around his shoulder.

'Nivver!' Axe cried and pointed
            to the musicians who
had gathered behind him
like ripe fruit
behind sheltering leaves.
'These guys are ready tae jam,
this is ma band

            – I shall nivver surrender!'

Where are the fox-holes of Paradise?
   Aye, where's the fox?
Buddha clapped his hands
and danced
in the sweltering heat
to the shattered beat
where timbril, oud and drums resounded
the logic behind the logos
of that great square that's not a square
yet translates as *Place of wandering spirits...*
At length Buddha knelt and gently placed
his very favourite bandana
round our Axe's sweating neck.
   Thank you, friend.

Stella and the Monkey-man

We left Brock there
as the crowd thickened like soup in the pot
around a stir of story-tellers
that in song, mime and patter cooked up
one of the world's three oldest stories:
rich man, poor man, rich man's daughter
– pausing only for water and passing the hat.

   I recommend the Monkey-man, who plays
   the sultan's daughter, the flirt!

(Thank you, no
hashish will be necessary tonight)
His tawdry skirt, burlesque rouge,
vermilion lips on wrinkled skin
may seem pitiable, or an easy laugh,
* – but look.*
Look into his Eyes.

                    – A shock, isn't it.

As the crowd circles
    like the nozzle of a bellows
and drums and pipes puff lust
    and the rich man rages
and the poor man dreams,
    the Monkey-man's a glowing coal
igniting ancillary fires
    in every man and woman there.
And as he minces, sighs, winks,
    humps the air and shamelessly
turns on the crowd,
    he seems to say

        Yes: monkey we are
        monkey we be...

    – 'Oh wicked eyes, oh innocent palms!'
    our Stella cried.
    'I have felt nothing in two years.
    I have mislaid the outstanding
    like a face in the crowd.
    Now I must follow him.'

The Monkey-man held out his tambourine.
She flicked her hair back from her eyes,
took it
        and followed
and red puffs
rose from their sandals
as they hurried through the dusk...

No, let her go. That part of you must go
down into the night with the Monkey-man.
Without feeling, the poet's world's in chaos.
He will not harm her,
                    just become her for a while.

Suppose I could handle some plain prose
for a day or two.
She'll be all right?

She comes to bits, he'll fuse her.
That spikey, tough and oh so
fragile woman glows
like a filament in argon
and each bulb yearns
for the moth that can break it.

She never did want happiness,
that ordinary quest.
She will return?

Dazed, singed, amnesiac perhaps.
These night trips cost.
Her Art wants knowledge,
but she still wants it free.
She won't return the same
        down the tremmelin road of flame.

Dearie me,
these modern muses walk the wild side.
But still my heart runs after her
like a gleikit pup-dog, yelping.
I'll keep a candle burning.

Tonight your Axe-man rocks the kasbah,
Grimpeur disputes with the Immam,
– let's me and you
        eat roast chestnuts
as a new moon rises
                over the Koutabia,
then catch the last bus to the coast.

Stella after the Monkey-Man

Being is a flame
steady in the corner of a monastery
or roaring on a stage
before ten thousand other torches

My hair is black
My eyes are black
I have clasped the Monkey-man
I am pure as charcoal

Grass is a flame
Trees burn under their bark
A dead cow by the road
combusts within

People are upright flames
legs arms head
the five-branched candelabra
conceived on beds of fire

I have gone down with the Monkey-man
and he has taught me how to see:

the stars are flaming
the bunsens are all burning in the lab tonight
all across the universe lights are blazing

Welcome home
it's terribly wasteful
but that's the way of it

Tonight no one is breathing
except in flames

the beggar leans
on a stick of flames
the yogi's groin
is a nest of flames

Yet desire's the very least of it

I fear nothing
for these dark ways
are lit at intervals
by scurrying torches

for I have donned the Monkey-man
and he has taught me how to see

On the bus

…Your company have gone before,
further down their separate ways,
there's nothing further for you here
and it ain't polite to linger gawping.
Time soon to be sailing
back to your ain.

But take a month off,
a sort of Interlude before the final act.
Rent the tower in the Villa Maroc,
write up your journals and attend
to the spirit lurking in the fact.
Get yourself work, approach
the skeelie skippers of this salt-glazed town.
See where they lounge like partans,
hard-skinned upon their dazzling nets.

* * *

Would ya take a look
  at my story so far
    while I go for coffees?

– Ya beezer, I!
It's thick enough to crush a crustacean.
Where you going for these coffees – Casablanca?

INTERLUDE IN ESSAOUIRA

We always knew there'd be a place
where North Atlantic winds converge
on Africa as we went down
for sardines and cigarettes among the nets
with Abdul, Hervé, Mr James,
and after work there would be time
for mint tea and talk in the Place Moulay Hassan
where women in haik sit like pillars of salt
and hooded men stroll hand in hand
by children rapt on the mosaics...

We knew dusk must adjust its shawl
by the Red Café, round the hammam,
and desert winds disturb those birds
hung in their cages in the hall.
'Soon all we've said and done will be
blown over the ocean without adieu' –
the residue glitters, like salt on the tiles,
in eyes with the sheen of windows, facing the sea.

The ship is waiting at the dock.
For a while
you'll be on your tod. Fear not.

PART V

**Bringing It All Back Home
(The Debatable Lands)**

The wanderer returns – King of the Scots? – a Fantastic Cloak –
a Brocken Spectre – the Debatable Lands – Praises – Journey's
end, lovers meeting – an early retirement? – Homburg! – The
Return of the Heretical Buddha – fast by an ingle – the Courts
of the Stourie Feet

THE WANDERER RETURNS

Waves accelerate towards the beach
like grief they break when shallowest.
A black sail
is leaving Dalriada.

Your man staggers from the water
claws into the sand.
He lies motionless till dawn
in the small rain.
It's like a flat battery
re-charging at the mains.

   That evening
on the hilltop where
his Western ancestors looked out
he slowly fits his foot
into the hollow in the rock.
'Omnes aut nemo', he murmurs,
holds his arms aloft:
'King of the Scots'.

   – Well, why not?
Everyone's gotta be someone
and sure as fate
in this wee country
I must be related.

He waits in that high crowning place
till the company rise and clasp
around him like a cloak

woven from earth and fire and air,
glittered with salt from the Western Ocean,
dyed from deep bracken and high empty moor,
and yellow lichen from the auld fell dyke,
smoothed by waves' green sook –
ach! it is material as tweed,
coarse, close-woven, rough on skin yet
light as peat smoke from the far side of the glen,
subtle as the curlew pirl-pirling
silence back upon itself above the furthest cairn.

Strange cloth for sure
but we're raised to it.
As this era blows out like a storm,
we surely gonna need it.

Wrapped in that fabled cloak,
that ancient and modern
tormenting Nessus' shirt, that coat
of many tongues and colours,
whose wide lapels are Western Isles
to one side, Caithness to the other,
    whose central belt draws tight,
whose pockets hold Berwick and Dumfries,
    whose skirts spread wide about the Borders,
whose ragged cowl's Shetlandic, whose collar
    ruffs the low green fields of Orkney –

he is ready now to clasp his Company:
    singed Stella, auld hirpling Brock
    and brooding Ken still bearing the sheath,
each with their knowledge and their injuries
for knowledge and injury birl together
'like water going over the mill-wheel'...

    'I can see at last,'
    she said, 'into anyone's heart
    now I've forever lost my own.'
    She opened her cloak and showed
    below her rosy-tipped left breast
    a long black slanting scar.
    'The Monkey-man's price like Cruachan
    was steep
                but fair.
    It's what I wanted.'

    They drew closer together,
my flickering shards.

'In this country, at this time,'
Ken said, 'if you haven't anger,
you've got nothing.
                And if
all you've got is anger
you really have got nothing.
Take the rubble of my thought
and mak a kirk or a mill o it,
but something honest, hamely, decent.
Embrace me, friends.'

On that hilltop they embraced,
drew round like a masoned wall
till none could slip a dirk atween them
and the circle like an ancient brooch
was unbroken in the setting sun.

'Jings, yon's a blinnin stew!'
Brock cried. 'The years
flee like driven snaw and I
could get emotional.
Let's hie
                far from this turbulent place!
The body drags and yet
ma days burn doon wi'oot regret –
oor loyalty's now tae the pack
no tae the cigarette.'
And he stood on Dunadd,
body-black against the setting sun
and wi the haill voice
pledged allegiance yet again
to sex & stress & rock 'n roll –
all the goodies flesh is heir to
when to its kingdom comes
that brief sweet tormented reign –

and they saw not the thickening body of a brute
but an anthracite jewel of a man
flaming in an earthly setting.

*

They lay on warm slabs above the sea
                                            and the wind
                                            dropped with the
                                            sun

and gazed until the corrugations of the brain
'smoothed to one broad blaze',
then wordless slipped into
their common sleeping bag
and finally
            they
                slept
                        as
                            One

A Parting Song

Across the land
trees lean to the East,
they bend with the prevailing wind
and never ask for peace.
And when I woke
dew-soaked and alone
that was the way to go.

I looked back once
and it made me grue
for in that morning's mist and sun
a dark figure gestured
one hundred feet high,
a freak of weather,
light lancing from
the heart of the storm:

   a Brocken Spectre
waving so long

IN THE DEBATABLE LANDS

From the top of Rest and Be Thankful
where glaciers had once ground down
like ancient grudges,
    I saw the bare hills
    and I saw the conifered hills
    and I saw the submarine base
    and all its brambly wire
and I didna ken
if I was looking at my ain belle countrie
or a disaster zone.

And I stravaiged through the Lowlands
where the lights were blazing
but precious few were at home
and I wasn't one of them.

And as I wandered
with full rucksack and an empty sheath
I tried to figure what the game was
and had we lost or won.

So I turned South
to the headwaters of the Tweed
and camped by Liddiesdale
in the heart of the Debatable Lands.

*

    Still don't know what I was
waiting for – revelation maybe –
but still the many voices of my land
hissed like drizzle on the tent
as I lay listening
for the ordering within...

Small veins beat on the back of your hand   *Rivers*
                                                                         run down
                                                                           through the
                                                                         night

(and if I was half-cracked
it was in the way of a kernel
ripe to fall from its shell)

stars and cobwebs hang together
                                        above
                                    the lily–
                                        choked
                                        burn

and by their light I read
lines scratched on the sheath
in *ogham*, a Pictish script that said

[....||||||.....]

(untranslatable...)

I lay against the standing stone
hard by the ruined keep
where pee-weets
like thoughts made black and white
tilted and were gone...

the Kingdom is already spread upon the Earth
only men can't read it

and my mind went back and forth across the border
until one night there was a blue
amphitheatre of clouds round the moon
and naked   speechless   unarmed
I rose through that arena –

I opened my eyes
   Impossible to say
      what had changed

but each pebble, grass and curlew cry
   seemed weighted
      as if it shyly bore within

all existence rising.
   I saluted the morning
      and packed my tent.

Headwaters

Today one can only trace
the headwaters of the Tweed.

The waters are real water
however much they won't hold
still to be told
exactly where they begin.

The earth is the real earth,
there is no other
so cold on the fingers
so close to the bone.

And these trees are real trees
not pale counters on the map.
And the loud city of men talking crap
and the busy city of women moving on

      is the real city of women and men
      in a perpetual state of arousal
      for there is more there to desire
      than anyone can possibly possess
      so even the rich itch with suspicion
      they may be missing something
      and the poor are bloody sure they are.

And so in a way the city is
the perfect lover,
the one who never quite delivers
which is smack on line for those
still young or healthy or simply
hungry enough to love
the addiction more than the drug.
And the woman standing at the corner

tan suitcase in her hand
thinks there's a choice here
between a bed-sit and the nearest bar
when into her head slides a picture
of a place where there are stones
        never cut for tenements
and she stands
dumfounert in the autumn rain...

Veins beat down the back of her hand
as burns flow into one another.

* * *

I wandered North along the coast,
hitched a boat across the river,
turned East for home
('the kingdom is already spread...')

All the while, 'gainst rain and sun
I wore Bud's quirky panama,
a black hat with a silver band,
and I took it off for no one

till in a quiet street in Fife
I met a drookit woman with a suitcase
and she quite clearly wore
a black band on a silver hat

and we both stopped, mid-gest –

BUD: *'The final move's*
from mythic gypsy derring-do
to the domestic
                    and so
redeem it
            and
end up as we must
living daily
            earthly wonders'

KEN: *A knife, however dual, is just*
        a fine example of a blade...

STELLA: *The Blade's no phallic power source*
            but a tool for use about the house,
                baring a wire
            or in the kitchen, cutting bread...

And deep in the body
I heard Brock *laugh.*

AN EARLY RETIREMENT?

The Quest seemed over.
The Company had wed awa.
I more or less forgot about the Buddha –
these things happen: busy.

For that woman with the complimentary panama
and I went back to Pittenweem and Anster
and she knew where the boundaries were –
Some things fit: naturally.

I hung the sheath above the mantel
among the photos of the Himal
packed the axes in the attic
with Stell's head-scarf and Ken's theses,

Bud's nifty panama and belt and braces –
all things become: yesterday and vatic.

THE RETURN OF THE HERETICAL BUDDHA

I'd simply gone for fish suppers
when I saw one I knew,
   strolling the Folly
   as the summer shows assembled.
I clapped him on the back.
                       'Homburg!'
(I cried him) 'Your overcoat is still too lang.
Where you been syne?'
He shrugged. *Aw, teaching, ken.*

Big Brudder sat on Anster harbour wall
and spat. *Fans will be fans*, he sighed,
though I sometimes wish they wouldn't.

He wore a black bernous, which was becoming
worthy of note by the regular citizens,
but at least, as he remarked, it was *becoming.*
Seagulls wheeled about his head,
dust motes danced around his sandals
but he seemed wearit as he checked me oot.

A fine hardening, he said at last.
*Come park your arse upon this wall.
We can have talk, or the other.*

Bud leaned against the Hannah Harvey light,
surveyed the crowd on Shore Street.
So little surgery, so many scars.
He cracked his knuckles, scaffed
a cigarette, struck the match on his pate.

   'Whit ails ya, Buddha?'

Nae particular scunners, kid.
He dragged on appearance, coughed up
reality, sighed.

The silly sheep keep their heads down
and end up grilled with new potatoes.
It will soon be time to die again.
Anyone who can be enlightened
is enlightened. As for your Quest –

   'Yes? My hair is grey,
   my companions are gone,
   I feel okay but
   still don't hold the Blade.
   So how about some Good News?'

He licked his thumb
and held it to the breeze
and all the satellite dishes of the town
turned in his direction
and the viewers saw strange things
until the thumb dried
and he lowered it
with a very wee grin.

   'Call this wisdom?' I cried
   'Let's go to the Happy Haddock
   if you've no better fish to fry.'

– He flung his arms wide
like shutters opening above
a mighty bluff
   that gives out over
      glimpsed endless ocean:

      Then all along the fatal coast
tides rose and fell like rapid breath.
Along the High Street letters flowed
   in and out the post box, a blur
as generations were posted
   here and there across the universe
each sealed in envelopes of skin,
           the saddest
unopened and unread.

                         Shadows
struggled to their feet,
toddled, ran, collided,
            opened arms and opened legs
once, twice,
then fell back into the earth exhausted.
The howf was a saddler's was a café
was a launderette then
a Craft Shoppe and
a thousand years of fishermen
downed oilskins and auditioned
for walk-on parts with East Neuk Heritage...

Matter, he sighed, *is condemned*
to eternal push-ups and goodbyes.
Everything
               is nothing mostly
even your physicists know that.
You must learn to think bifocal
to focus on
                    what's nearest
                    and the distant view.
    I advise you to ignore the middle ground,
anything within the range
of newspapers.
                Don't buy
what can be bought –
it's rubbish.
Without expectation, aid all living things.
And my opinion of life remains
probably the least interesting thing about it.

    He took a last drag,
carefully flicked the cig away
fizzling across the rooftops like a smart bomb
till it fell in the wasteland
known locally as 'Little Africa'
(and from that dowp
great spliffs sprang up,
plucked still at the full moon
by local quines and loons
in matching silver jackets

who stitched upon their Colours bear
in midnight blue:
                    'The Beggar's Benison'
and 'The Maiden's Prayer'...)
I'm deid done, I tell ya.
Bear me to the foothills of the Himalaya
and leave me there till I forget.

Ananda, most loyal of my companions,
(yet always slightly dumb
in spiritual matters), the one
who persuaded me on the admission of nuns,
let's hyne awa. The pines of my childhood
twitch through long-gone afternoons,
I should be there.

    He walked to the pier edge,
took a last look at Anster,
and his lang neb minded me of my faither,
recently deceased. He touched
my shoulder. *Goodbye.*
    Oh aye –
I think this blade is yours.

    He handed me
the small tartan penknife
A PRESENT FROM AYR
I'd picked up at the start.

I think you'll find it sharp enough.

    Then he turned his back,
held out his arms again and cried
Come, Ananda! Let us go to Kusinagara!
    One push and he was gone.
I picked up his bernous,
put the knife in my pooch
and went home.

'Where you been
for those fish suppers,
darlin – Kyle of Lochalsh?'

'Big Qs at the Happy Haddock,'
I said, and grinned because a penknife,
however tartan, is still at best
just a fine instance of a blade
(and I knew the Stella part in me
living and breathing
as I lived and breathed,
always distant, always on hand,
and as a shower of sparks went down my heart
it was not so much alchemical
wedding as a *welding*)

That's why he'd handed me
what I had always had,
and the woman before me (licking her fingers)
was the finest instance of a human
that I was ever likely
to be so lucky
as to always and to ever and to never.

And somewhere, Stella *smiled*.

*

It was my 40th year and my first child
was growing in that hungry woman
whose left hip I swear
repeated the curve
of the field above the house where I was born:

I hung my boots by the ingle
thumbed the blade, sharpened a pencil,
took out the journals
sat by the fire
and looked into the flames for a while.

If you cannot bring good

It's a burning world
wherever you stand.
(Who are these figures with torches?
Where are they taking us?)
Bud knew that, we ken that
who live in debatable lands.
(Look into those flames,
what do you see?)

If you cannot bring good news

We are right to be afraid
who do not know the meaning of this
who do not know where we are being taken
who are swept through the dark
never seeing the faces
that hold the torches.
And where will we find courage?

then don't bring any

Born of dust
swept down the roads
even the householders
have no permanent home.
We red-eyed vaigs,
waifs, tinklers, strays,
escorted by fire
we have come at last
to the *Court of the Stourie Feet*.
And what will the judgement be?

waves beat
upon an empty shore

KEN'S GLOSSARY, NOTES & ACKNOWLEDGEMENTS

PART I: The Quest & The Company

Men On Ice was the precursor of *Western Swing*. It concerned the doings of three climbers of a sort (Poet, Axe-Man and Grimpeur, plus The Bear) upon a mountain of sorts. It had many of the qualities and themes of its time (mid 70s)

guddle: to catch with the hands by groping underwater; to do things in a careless, slovenly way.

a haiver: a person who talks nonsense, usually at length.

'Scotland. January. Snow': this crossing of Rannoch to the Clachaig Inn reappears in *Electric Brae*, from which come the climbers and a prototype of Stella.

doo-lally: a bit crazy.

Communicado: an excellent Glasgow-based theatre company.

forfochen: exhausted, especially with fighting.

Gerard de Nerval: the poet who took his lobster for a walk, hung himself in the rue de la Vieille Lanterne in Paris (*see* Richard Holmes' *Footsteps*).

'...the surgeons stand...': this phrase is lifted from a fine poem by David Scott of Gourock, whose 'Now Close Your Eyes' poem is a template for 'A Cure for Loneliness'.

Sampling: a technique in music production where a snippet of a song – too short to infringe copyright – is lifted and digitally pasted onto an original backing track. Alternatively one may sample from a few notes of a voice or instrument its particular tone, transfer that sound into a digital synthesiser, and then play a new melody which employs that tone. An example here would be the 'cadence replication' of Pound's *'and the old sarcophagi, such as lie, smothered in grass by San Vitale'* (from Canto 1) used here to sign off Part II. There are several such replications here and a deal of sampling, conscious and unconscious, from poetry and more frequently from song lyrics, the literacy of a generation. The sampling techniques herein owe much to Eliot-Pound who developed the first modern sequencer. Some of their mixes are here sampled in turn. Sampling is not however a recent phenomenon – artists through all ages have borrowed, referred, pastiched and re-worked their tradition and contemporaries for their own purposes.

Stella's Letter samples from Lou Reed's *Sweet Jane*, Robin Williamson's *The Yellow Snake*, Talking Heads, Dylan's *Mr Tambourine Man*, Chris Isaac's *Western Stars*, Henryson's *The Testament of Cresseid*, *The Twa Corbies*, *River Deep, Mountain High*, MacDiarmid's *The Drunk Man Looks at the Thistle*, Jesus and Mary Chain's *Dark-*

lands, The Byrds, *Clockwork Orange*, and of course the sampling in Part V of *The Waste Land*.

Brownsbank: the Borders home of Hugh MacDiarmid.

'...And when the Buddha sat' and **'and the mighty earth thundered...':** from Joseph Campbell's *Occidental Mythology*.

forjeskit, wabbit: worn out, exhausted; **gallus:** bold, wild, unmanageable; **dreich:** dreary, dark, tiresome; **blate:** bashful, modest.

'Je me lance vers la gloire': from Talking Heads' *Psycho Killer*.

The Night Watchman comes from Dylan's *Visions of Johanna*, as do the binoculars on page 56.

reive: to plunder or pillage.

Ken's Fax contains a confused reference to Bateson's *Notes Towards an Ecology of Mind*.

PART II: The Up & Down Disco

The Up & Down Disco was the most sweaty, sleazy and sordid night club in Kathmundu. Its decor was red and black and windowless, its clientele are described. A favoured haunt of Himalayan climbers, it is now regrettably closed.

Namaste: a Tibetan-Nepali greeting, blessing, salutation.

'The beers went down...' is from a story by Ros Brackenbury.

Western Swing: a form of Country music incorporationg elements of jazz, Blues and Mexican music. Its use here is broader and looser, perhaps to indicate the Western style, mentality, mind.

'soft angora night' and **'let us pass out praises...'** sample from poems by Kathleen Jamie.

birlin: turning, dancing.

'your desire to perpetuate these nymphs...' – see Mallarmé's *L'Après-Midi d'un Faune*.

A Remarkably Obscene Sonnet: monsoon rain washed away the only copy.

'the haill clanjamfrie': *see* MacDiarmid's *Bonnie Broukit Bairn*.

laasi: a fruit and yoghurt drink popular in Nepal.

The band from East Kilbride are The Jesus and Mary Chain, and *A Million Rainy Days* is theirs.

dwam: a daydream, a trance.

Cham: Chamonix, a centre of Alpinism.

'and consequently smelt like Heaven': from Jonathan Richman's *Roadrunner*.

greit: to cry; **sonsie:** pleasant, cheery, honest.

'A mooth you could post a haddock in': a haiver or blabbermouth.

thrawn: perverse, obstinate.

PART III: Travails in the High Atlas

'Dust on our bags and our capes' is lifted from Dylan's *Romance in Durango*.

flegsome: frightening; dumfounert: dumfounded, bewildered.

'This dawn is not my enemy's' – *see* 'Dissenting Passages' from *Surviving Passages*.

'heartbreak adjusting her sandal': 'I' is probably picturing the statue of Athene known as 'Victory adjusting her sandal'.

neb: nose; machair: land by the shore covered with bent-grass.

'When I was young we had two pear trees...': see 'Grimpeur and the Yobs' from *Men On Ice*. This line, like the origins of that book, came from a school French reader, e.g. 'No, your tie is too gaudy'.

'Pear blossoms drifted...': in this scene 'I' is likely thinking of 'The blossoms of the apricot blow from the East to the West...' the close of Pound's XIII Canto.

Allt a' Mhuilinn: the burn running from the great Northern corrie of Ben Nevis.

'...Turtles all the way down': this comes from *New Scientist* by way of illustrating how the universe can be at once bounded and infinite, or perhaps boundless and finite.

'Deep dark secret river...': this stanza comes recollected from a manuscript poem by Sean Kane of Trent University, Ontario.

'Fast by an angle' is a nip from *Tam O'Shanter*.

hirpling: limping; speir: ask, enquire; a munelicht flittin: to move house hurriedly and secretly to avoid debts.

A MacDiarmidtron is an early synthesiser (cf. the mellotron that introduces *Strawberry Fields Forever*) that shifts linguistic register to a dense Scots from many parts and periods. Best decoded (and sometimes created) by a *Jamieson's Dictionary of the Scottish Language*. Prime cuts are MacD's early short lyrics and *The Drunk Man*. See also Sydney Goodsir Smith.

leid: language, tongue; keek: glance, peep; fairlies: wonders; blaw: blast; lift: the sky, air; aiblins: perhaps; wheechin: hurrying; airt: direction, place, art; stravaig: to wander, ramble; dree my weird: endure my fate; a gemme o toolies: a game of marbles.

'The Earth's a bride...birlin there': this densely sequences Dave Edmonds' *I Knew the Bride (When she used to Rock 'n' Roll)* with MacD's *Bonnie Broukit Bairn* and The Beatles' *I Saw Her Standing There*. The tune of 'And aa the bricht stars...' is Hamish Henderson's *Freedom Come All Ye*.

The 'curious motif': Eddie Irwin of Tara Trust and the Samye

Ling Monastery pointed this out.

'Duel...jewelry': not sure I entirely follow Stell's logic here.

'One star awake' is I think the ending of the Irish song *She Walked Through the Fair*.

PART IV: In Marrakech (Narratives of Desire)

The Djemma el Fna is the great central square (though it isn't) in Marrakech: theatre, market, preachers' and hustlers' paradise.

'All narratives are narratives of desire' is a reworking of a line from Ron Butlin's *Then and Now*.

'One fer the money': Carl McPerkins, *c*.1957.

wersh: bitter.

'the sultan's dawg': this mysterious fragment broke away from **'the sultan's daughter'** (page 82) and reappeared on the screen for page 80 as a ghost image.

'his hands in his pockets...': a bent sample from Dylan's *Fourth Time Around*.

'where timbril, oud and drums resound': a reworking of Ron Butlin's *Fellow Travellers*.

'the crowd thickened...': this line came from Peter Drahoney in Dundee 1970. Where are you now, Pete?

gleikit: daft, stupid, foolish.

The **Villa Maroc** in Essaouira is an extraordinary guest house where this longpoem started at 3 a.m., waking with the words 'I am afraid'. Thanks to Mr James Whaley for the Tower Room there.

partans: crabs.

PART V: Bringing It All Back Home (The Debatable Lands)

The Debatable Lands are the historically disputed borderlands round Liddiesdale.

Dalriada was the original West coast of Scotland kingdom of the Scotti who left Ireland to colonise and name Scotland, finally under the leadership of Kenneth MacAlpine crushing the Picts who then disappeared from history.

'fits his foot...': on top of Dunadd hill, overlooking Dalriada, is a foot-shaped hollow in the rock where reputedly the new leader of the Scotti placed his foot to establish his authority.

'I must be related': cf. 'We're aa Jock Tamson's bairns'.

'like water going over the mill-wheel': Pound, Stella thinks.

Cruachan: the imposing mountain overlooking the Pass of Brander.

'In this country...got nothing' was said by Isobel Wylie in Leith after another General Election.

'**Wi the haill voice**' is the title of Edwin Morgan's translations of Mayakovsky. This poem owes much to his élan and innovative energy.

'**and the wind...one broad blaze**' re-works Norman MacCaig's *Tea-Break by Loch Assynt*.

grue: shudder, shiver.

Rest and Be Thankful: is the high pass on the A82 between Beinn Ime and Beinn an Lochain.

'**still don't know what I was waiting for**': the opening of Bowie's *Changes*.

Ogham is the Pictish script. It remains untranslatable.

pee-weets: lapwings.

The woman with the suitcase steps from Lou Reed's *Sweet Jane*.

'**the final move's...**' and '**no phallic power source...**': a comment on an early version, by Rory Watson of Stirling University.

'**stones never cut for tenements**' is a line from Robert Alan Jamieson.

drookit: drenched; **vatic**: just one of those words.

'**two fish suppers...**' this passage samples Eliot's 'Stetson' with Procul Harum's *Homburg*, in a confusion of hats.

The Folly, originally 'Rodger's Folly', is part of the shore front of Anstruther (Anster) harbour. The Hannah Harvey lighthouse is at the end of the West Pier.

scunner: sickness, dislike, problem, boredom.

The surreal post-box borrows from Lennon's *Across the Universe*.

East Neuk Limited was set up to market the East Neuk of Fife. Its symbol was an at least life-size fibreglass 'fisher lassie', who can still be seen inside the Murray Library, Shore Street.

'**Without expectation aid...**': this concept of useful compassion as the only pure motivation for pursuing enlightenment is very much that of Akong Rinpoche's at the Samye Ling monastery, and the HB owes something to him.

'**Little Africa**' does exist, though it takes a bit of finding.

Ananda was traditionally Gautama Buddha's body-servant, closest companion, disciple, while being slightly slow on the spiritual up-take, the last of that circle to attain enlightenment, and the one who persuaded him to permit an order of Buddhist nuns. For these reasons I like him.

Kusinagara: towards the end of his life, the Buddha returned with Ananda to the area of his birth in the hills of Northern India.

'**If you cannot bring good news...**': from Dylan's *The Wicked Messenger*.

The Court of the Stourie Feet was the court held by the gypsies/tinkers/vaigs/travellers or stourie-fuit ('dusty feet') to dispense justice and settle arguments.

These Notes & Acknowledgements owe something to Grimpeur's innovative Glossary/Index in *Men On Ice*, and echo similar devices in Alasdair Gray's works, and re-work with just a tinge of irony Eliot's *The Waste Land* notes which too explained a few things, invited further reading: and helped make up the required number of pages.

This text may suggest not so much a kleptomaniac with a bad memory as an attempt to acknowledge, respect and harness the plurality (literary, linguistic, artistic and social) of a culture and a generation.

Swing low, sweet carrion crow